1st EDITION

HOW TO SEE THE PROPHET MUHAMMAD _{PBUH} IN DREAMS

THREE REAL STORIES

FOR ALL PEOPLE WHO HOPE TO SEE THE LAST ALLAH'S MESSENGER _{PBUH}

By Doctor
Abdeslam HAMRANI

Verification

The linguistic content was verified by Mr. **Mohamed ESSBAI**, Teacher of English, and Responsible of Postgraduate Service at Ibn Tofaïl University in Morocco.

The Islamic content was verified by Mr. **Larbi KARKOURI**, Teacher of English, Imam for Friday prayers, and Preacher at some mosques in Kenitra, Morocco.

Contents

Preface	7
Introduction	9
Prophet Muhammad	11
Prophet viewing	15
Sleep	*15*
Dreams	*15*
Real steps	*17*
Verse of the Throne	21
Chapter of the Purity of Faith	25
Chapter of the Glorious Morning Light	27
Real stories on the prophet viewing	29
First viewing	31
Second viewing	35
Third viewing	37
Benefits of the prophet viewing	39
Conclusion	41
References	43
List of texts	45

Preface

Praise be to Allah who has favored us and made us Muslims, followers of the greatest prophet Muhammad peace be upon him *(PBUH)*. All the blessings and Allah's salutations are upon our Messenger, his family, his companions, and all his followers up to the Day of Judgment.

Seeing the prophet *PBUH* in dream is a dear wish that every Muslim has. Many virtuous Muslims have seen him many times. He even solved their problems.

When Imam Malik was writing his book "Al-Muwatta", the prophet *PBUH* came to him in dream and said to him: "Watti'ho", which means: "simplify it".

Imam Al-Ghazali said that he was teaching, and he was proud to be a great scholar and to have such a big number of students who were themselves scholars. One of the students rose and said: "Allah Most High said: Every day He is (engaged) in some affair" *(55 Ar-Rahman 29)*. What is He doing now?

The Imam had no answer, so he said: "I will answer you tomorrow". But the following day, the student asked for the answer and the Imam still had none. That evening the Imam did his ablutions, prayed some rakaats, then sent a lot of prayers to the prophet Muhammad *PBUH*, and did a lot of invocations before he went to bed. In his sleep, he had a dream. The prophet *PBUH* came to him in dream and told him: "Tell your student that Allah has things that He shows but doesn't begin (Everything is already done in His knowledge –

Everything is written in the Board – He shows them at the right time). He raises the ranks of some people, and He lowers some others".

The following day, the Imam said: "Where is the person who asked me about what Allah is doing?" The student said: "Here I am". The Imam gave him the answer that the prophet $_{PBUH}$ had given him. And to the imam's surprise, the student said: "Pray upon he who had taught you (i.e. the prophet $_{PBUH}$).

The Imam Qortoby said: "Viewing the prophet $_{PBUH}$ in any time is possible. It is a truth from God, but it does not necessitate being free from sins. Its content can be tidings about a good end of life, or dying on the state of belief, or it can be a warning in order to be away from sins. The prophet companions saw him in dreams and in day dreams without being free from sins".

The prophet $_{PBUH}$ said: "He who sees me in dream, it is as if he sees me in reality because Satan cannot disguise himself in me" *(Muslim 2266, Abu Dawud 5023, Ahmad 5/306)*.

O Allah, Help us all see in dream the Messenger that you have sent to us. Help us have a trip to his mosque so that we can greet him directly there where he lies. Make us so lucky to enjoy his intercession. And make us so lucky to be his close companions in Paradise with "those on whom Allah has bestowed His Grace of the prophets, the Siddiqun (those followers of the prophets who were first and foremost to believe in them like Abu Bakr As-Siddiq $_{may\ Allah\ be\ pleased\ with\ him}$), the martyrs and the righteous" *(4 An Nissa'b 69)*. And make us enjoy seeing Your Face. You are able to do all things.

Mr. **Larbi KARKOURI**
Teacher of English, Imam for Friday prayers, and Preacher at some mosques.

Introduction

In the name of Allah, most Gracious, most Merciful, we start introducing this book about the viewing of the prophet Muhammad peace be upon him *(PBUH)* in dreams. Seeing the prophet *PBUH* is the biggest concern of all Muslims. Personally, I have hoped to see the prophet *PBUH* in my dreams, and receive his blessings. For me, seeing Him *PBUH* in dreams is a proof of the faithful behavior.

Telling people about the steps I took to see the prophet *PBUH* is the main aim of the present work. Three real and true stories are written to help people who hope seeing the prophet Muhammad *PBUH*, remember Allah Most High, and the last life. The person who hopes seeing Him *PBUH* should follows some rituals during the day. This seeing is one of the good and true dreams or in Arabic "Ru'aya".

Before describing what I did to see the prophet Muhammad *PBUH*, I would like to present a brief notice about:

- Birth, wives, and children of the prophet Muhammad *PBUH*;
- Dreams classification and steps of prophet *PBUH* viewing in dreams during sleep;
- Showing the recited text in Arabic of the:
  o Verse of the Throne;
  o Chapter of the Purity of Faith;
  o Chapter of the Glorious Morning Light.

After that, we will describe and explain the real and true stories on the prophet *PBUH* viewing, and its benefits.

Finally, we hope you will be able to see the prophet *PBUH* several times in your dreams during your life, and accompany Him *PBUH* in the Firdaws Paradise after death.

Prophet Muhammad

The prophet Muhammad $_{PBUH}$ is the last Allah's messenger, He $_{PBUH}$ was sent to guide his Ummah to the correct way.

The prophet $_{PBUH}$ is a witness for the believers on the Day of Judgment. Allah in the Quran says that the prophet Muhammad $_{PBUH}$ was sent only as a "Mercy to the entire Universe". All thanks and praises are due to Allah Most High. May peace and blessings be upon the prophet Muhammad $_{PBUH}$, his family, his companions, and those who follow his tradition [1].

The prophet Muhammad $_{PBUH}$ was born in Macca, Saoudi Arabia, on Monday Rabi I 12th the elephant year (April 22nd 571 AD), after Jesus ascended into heaven to await his return before the end of the world [2]. His mother, Aminah, was the daughter of Wahb Ibn Abdu Manaf of the Zahrah family. His father, Abdullah, was the son of Abdul Muttalib. Muhammad's father died before his birth. His mother died before he reached the age of six years old, so the prophet Muhammad $_{PBUH}$ was put under the charge of his grandfather Abdul Muttalib who took the most tender care of him. But the old chief died two years afterwards. On his deathbed he confided to his son Abu Talib the charge of the little orphan [3].

The prophet $_{PBUH}$ lived in Macca, among his people, for forty years before the mission. This was the period of youth and manhood but he was ideal in everything, in his conduct, chastity, purity, honour and good manners [4].

Apart from the first marriage, the marriages of Allah's messenger *PBUH* were for the sake of religion and not for worldly pleasures. He firstly married the Lady Khadija who was elder than him; he was twenty-five years old and she was forty [4].

When Muhammad *PBUH* was twenty five years old, he traveled once more to Syria as a factor of a noble and rich Quraishi widow named Khadijah; and, having proved himself faithful in the commercial interests of that lady, he was soon rewarded with her hand in marriage [3].

After getting married, the prophet Muhammad *PBUH* had been accustomed to secluding himself in a cave in Hira Mount, a few miles away from Macca. The prophet *PBUH* used to go to this cave for meditation alone, sometime with his family. The Allah's divine inspiration touches Muhammad *PBUH* during one of those retirements and in the still hours of the night, an angel came to him to tell him that he was the Messenger of Allah Most High, sent to reclaim the fallen people to knowledge and the service of their Lord [3].

The prophet's wives *may Allah be pleased with them* are [5]:
- The Lady Khadijah Bint Khuwailid;
- The Lady Saudah Bint Zama'tun;
- The Lady Aisha Bint Abu Bakar;
- The Lady Hafsa Bint Umar;
- The Lady Zainab Bint Khuzaimah;
- The Lady Umm Salamah Bint Zaad Al-Raakib;
- The Lady Zainab Bint Jahsh;
- The Lady Juwairiyyah Bint Al-Harithy;
- The Lady Safiyah Bint Huyyah Bin Akhtab;
- The Lady Ramlah Bint Abu Sufyan;
- The Lady Maimunah Bint Alharithy Al-Hilalia;

- ...

The prophet $_{PBUH}$ had [4]:

- Four girls (Zainab, Omm Kalthoom, Fatima, Roqayya), and two boys (Abd Allah, Al Qassim) from the Lady Khadija;
- One boy from the Lady Maria called Ibrahim.

Remark: *The child Abd Allah is also called At-Tayyeb, and At-Tahir.*

Prophet viewing

Viewing the prophet Muhammad $_{PBUH}$ in dreams requires doing a ritual during the day before going to sleep. The sleep must be deep and with no high sounds. Because if the place of sleeping is not calm, the prophet $_{PBUH}$ viewing will not probably be realized.

A ritual was previously recommended and specified that the one who longs to see the prophet $_{PBUH}$ in dreams, should recite the verse of the Throne, the chapter of the Purity of Faith, and send, in the state of purification, blessings on the Holy Muhammad $_{PBUH}$ and his progeny [1].

1. Sleep

Sleep is a state of not being awake, a state of partial or full unconsciousness in people during which voluntary functions are suspended and the body rests and restores itself, or a period spent in this state [6].

2. Dreams

Dreams present all things that we see at the state of sleeping. They can be classified as of three kinds [7]:

- Good and true dreams: which come from Allah Most High;
- Evil dreams or nightmares: which come from Satan;
- Dreams that emanate from our own self.

Below three Hadiths from Sunna about the category of good and true dreams [7]:

- The prophet $_{PBUH}$ said: "Whoever sees me in a dream has really seen me, because Satan cannot appear in my image" *(Al-Bukhari, 5729)*;
- Narrated Anas bin Malik: Allah's Apostle said, "A good dream of a righteous person is one of forty-six parts of prophethood" *(Al-Bukhari)*;
- Narrated Ubada bin As-Samit: The Prophet said, "The good dreams of a faithful believer is a part of the forty-six parts of prophethood" *(Al-Bukhari)*.

Below two Hadiths about evil dreams which come from Satan [7]:

- Narrated Abu Sa'id Al-Khudri: I heard Allah's Apostle saying: "If anyone of you saw a dream which he liked, then that is from Allah, and he should thank Allah for it and tell it to others; but if he saw something else, i.e, a dream which he did not like, then that is from Satan and he should seek refuge with Allah from it and should not tell it to anybody, it will not harm him" *(Al-Bukhari)*;
- Narrated Abu Qatada: The Prophet said, "A true good dream is from Allah, and a bad dream is from Satan" *(Al-Bukhari)*.

Finally, the third kind of dreams from the self are of great importance since they constitute a very valuable yet private picture of the state or lack of health of our own inner being. Such dreams function, in fact, as windows to the soul [7].

3. Real steps

Seeing the prophet Muhammad $_{PBUH}$ is simple and easy if you do specific rituals such as reading some verses and chapters of the Holy Quran, helping people, remembering the names of Allah Most High and his prophet Muhammad $_{PBUH}$, doing invocations, being with good heart, etc.

In general, viewing the prophet requires following the way of the prophet Muhammad $_{PBUH}$. Personally, I tried to follow his way before that I saw Him $_{PBUH}$ in my dreams for three times. The real and true dreams give power and increase love and faith to Allah, and to his prophet Muhammad $_{PBUH}$.

Following all the manners of the prophet $_{PBUH}$ is very difficult, and nobody can follow him in anything without the grace and the help of Allah, especially in our days where the sins are so easy to be reached and done.

Doing sins by people is the main objective of the Satan. Therefore, we must be strong by asking the help of Allah Most High to stay away from sins during our life. The less sins are done, the more the dreams are true and real.

So as to see real dreams about the prophet Muhammad $_{PBUH}$, the person should say in the name of Allah and remember Him and His prophet $_{PBUH}$ before sleeping.

Below are some sentences that I always say during the day and before going to sleep:

- There is no God but Allah Most High;
- The prophet Muhammad is the Allah's messenger $_{PBUH}$;
- Muhammad is the Allah's prophet $_{PBUH}$;
- O my God Allah Most High, you are my love;
- O the prophet Muhammad $_{PBUH}$, you are my love;
- O Allah I want to see your beloved face;

- O Allah I want to enjoy your pardon on the day of judgment;
- Recitation of the verse of the Throne "Ayat Al-Kursi";
- Recitation of the chapter of the Purity of Faith "Surat Al-Ikhlas";
- Recitation of the chapter of the Glorious Morning Light "Surat Ad-Dhuha";
- …

Concerning the Quran recitation, I always recite the verse of the Throne for one single time, and the chapter of the Purity of Faith for three times directly on the Holy Quran in Arabic, before going to any place. I recite also the chapter of the Glorious Morning Light in Arabic with no specific time:

- I always read the verse of the Throne on the Holy Quran one single time before leaving home, or whenever I want to go out to any other place than home where I live. For example, if I want to go to the university, I read it one single time;
- After reading the verse of the Throne, I read the chapter of the Purity of Faith three times in Arabic, then I kiss the Quran. Afterwards, I ask Allah all good things that I want;
- I read another chapter of the Glorious Morning Light with no specific time when I come back home.

After recitation, I do invocations, and I ask Allah Most High anything such as help, success, respect, and being in the right way.

Reciting Quran and doing invocations are not sufficient to see the prophet Muhammad $_{PBUH}$. However, the person should be kind, helpful, and having a good heart. In other words, the person who hopes to see the prophet $_{PBUH}$ should follow the way of Allah and the manners of his prophet $_{PBUH}$. These are the essential ways for seeing the Holy Muhammad $_{PBUH}$ in dream during the state of sleep.

More the place of sleeping is calm, more the person will be blessed by seeing the prophet Muhammad $_{PBUH}$ if he or she follows the described steps as a daily practice.

Remark: *Touching the Quran book is permitted in the Islam only if the person is in a purification state.*

Verse of the Throne

The verse of the Throne is the verse 255 of the chapter of the Cow "al-Baqarah" in the Holy Quran [8].

I always recite the verse of the Throne (one single time), followed by the chapter of the Purity of Faith (three times) in Arabic directly on the Quran, and I kiss the Quran when I finish recitation. This ritual is repeated when I go out from home to any other place.

Remark: *The recitation of the verse of the Throne, for four times in Arabic is equivalent to all the Quran recitation.*

The verse of the Throne in Arabic is below:

ٱللَّهُ لَا إِلَٰهَ إِلَّا هُوَ ٱلْحَىُّ ٱلْقَيُّومُ لَا تَأْخُذُهُۥ سِنَةٌ وَلَا نَوْمٌ لَّهُۥ مَا فِى ٱلسَّمَٰوَٰتِ وَمَا فِى ٱلْأَرْضِ مَن ذَا ٱلَّذِى يَشْفَعُ عِندَهُۥٓ إِلَّا بِإِذْنِهِۦ يَعْلَمُ مَا بَيْنَ أَيْدِيهِمْ وَمَا خَلْفَهُمْ وَلَا يُحِيطُونَ بِشَىْءٍ مِّنْ عِلْمِهِۦٓ إِلَّا بِمَا شَآءَ وَسِعَ كُرْسِيُّهُ ٱلسَّمَٰوَٰتِ وَٱلْأَرْضَ وَلَا يَـُٔودُهُۥ حِفْظُهُمَا وَهُوَ ٱلْعَلِىُّ ٱلْعَظِيمُ ۝

Text 1: Verse of the Throne in Arabic.
(Chapter al-Baqarah 2: 255)

The verse of the Throne translated to English is below [8, 9]:

Allah! There is no god but He,-the Living, the Self-subsisting, Eternal. No slumber can seize Him nor sleep. His are all things in the heavens and on earth. Who is there can intercede in His presence except as He permitteth? He knoweth what (appeareth to His creatures as) before or after or behind them. Nor shall they compass aught of His knowledge except as He willeth. His Throne doth extend over the heavens and the earth, and He feeleth no fatigue in guarding and preserving them for He is the Most High, the Supreme (in glory).

Text 2: Verse of the Throne in English.
(Chapter al-Baqarah 2: 255)

In order to facilitate recitation of the verse of the Throne, I added the below text presenting Arabic pronunciation of this verse:

Allahu la ilaha illa Huwa, Alhayyu Lqayyum, la ta'khudhuhu sinatun wala nawm, lahu ma fi assamawati wama fil'ard, man dha alladhi yashfa'o indahu illa bi'idhnihi, ya'lamu ma bayna aydihim wa ma khalfahum, wala yuhituna bi shay'in min ilmihi illa bima sha'a, wasi'a kursiyyuhu assamawati wal ard, wala ya'uduhu hifdhuhuma, wa Huwa Laliyyu Ladheem.

Text 3: Arabic pronunciation of Throne verse.
(Chapter al-Baqarah 2: 255)

The benefits of reciting the verse of the Throne are announced in the Hadith [8]:

— Ubayy bin Ka'b *may Allah be pleased with him* reported: "The Messenger of Allah $_{PBUH}$ said: Abu Mundhir! Do you know which Ayah in Allah's Book is the greatest? I said: Allah and His messenger know best. He $_{PBUH}$

again said: Do you know which Ayah in Allah's Book is the greatest, according to you? I (Abu Mundhir) replied: It is Allah! There is no god but He - the Living, The Self-subsisting, Eternal" *(Muslim)*;

— Abu Hurairah *may Allah be pleased with him* narrated: "In Surah al-Baqaraah there is an ayah which is the best of all the ayahs of the Qur'an. It is never recited in a house but the Shaytan leaves: Ayat al-Kursi";

— "Do you know the Ayat al-Kursi? Anas *may Allah be pleased with him* replied I know. The Prophet *PBUH* said, It is equal to a quarter of the Qur'an".

Chapter of the Purity of Faith

The chapter of the Purity of Faith is the chapter 112 in the Holy Quran.

I always recite the chapter of the Purity of Faith three times after the verse of the Throne recitation in Arabic directly on the Holy Quran, and I kiss the Quran when I finish recitation. This practice is repeated whenever I go out from home to any other place.

Remark: *The recitation of the chapter of the Purity of Faith, for three times, in Arabic equal to all the Quran recitation.*

The chapter of the Purity of Faith in Arabic is below:

بِسْمِ ٱللَّهِ ٱلرَّحْمَٰنِ ٱلرَّحِيمِ

قُلْ هُوَ ٱللَّهُ أَحَدٌ ۝ ٱللَّهُ ٱلصَّمَدُ ۝ لَمْ يَلِدْ وَلَمْ يُولَدْ ۝ وَلَمْ يَكُن لَّهُۥ كُفُوًا أَحَدٌۢ ۝

Text 4: Chapter of the Purity of Faith in Arabic.
(Chapter 112)

The chapter of the Purity of Faith translated to English is below [9, 10]:

In the name of Allah, Most Gracious, Most Merciful. Say: He is Allah, the One and Only; Allah, the Eternal,

Absolute; He begetteth not, nor is He begotten; And there is none like unto Him.

Text 5: Chapter of the Purity of Faith in English.
(Chapter 112)

In order to facilitate recitation of the chapter of the Purity of Faith, I added the below text presenting Arabic pronunciation of this chapter:

Qul huwa Allahu ahad. Allahu assamad. Lam yalid wa lam yulad. Wa lam yakun lahu kofo'an ahad.

Text 6: Arabic pronunciation of the chapter of the Purity of Faith.
(Chapter 112)

The importance of reciting the chapter of the Purity of Faith is announced in Hadith [10]:

- According to Al-Bukhari, Abu Sa'id narrated that the Messenger of Allah said to his Companions: Is one of you not able to recite a third of the Qur'an in a single night? This was something that was difficult for them and they said, Which of us is able to do that, O Messenger of Allah? To which he replied, Allah al-Wahid as-Samad is a third of the Quran.

Chapter of the Glorious Morning Light

The chapter of the Glorious Morning Light is the chapter 93 in the Holy Quran [8].

I always recite some verses of the chapter of the Glorious Morning Light in Arabic and not directly on the Quran whenever I come back home with no specific time.

Remark: *The recitation of the chapter of the Glorious Morning Light is very important because it talks about the prophet Muhammad* PBUH.

The chapter of the Glorious Morning in Arabic is below:

بِسْمِ ٱللَّهِ ٱلرَّحْمَٰنِ ٱلرَّحِيمِ

وَٱلضُّحَىٰ ۝ وَٱلَّيْلِ إِذَا سَجَىٰ ۝ مَا وَدَّعَكَ رَبُّكَ وَمَا قَلَىٰ ۝ وَلَلْآخِرَةُ خَيْرٌ لَّكَ مِنَ ٱلْأُولَىٰ ۝ وَلَسَوْفَ يُعْطِيكَ رَبُّكَ فَتَرْضَىٰ ۝ أَلَمْ يَجِدْكَ يَتِيمًا فَـَٔاوَىٰ ۝ وَوَجَدَكَ ضَالًّا فَهَدَىٰ ۝ وَوَجَدَكَ عَآئِلًا فَأَغْنَىٰ ۝ فَأَمَّا ٱلْيَتِيمَ فَلَا تَقْهَرْ ۝ وَأَمَّا ٱلسَّآئِلَ فَلَا تَنْهَرْ ۝ وَأَمَّا بِنِعْمَةِ رَبِّكَ فَحَدِّثْ ۝

Text 7: Chapter of the Glorious Morning Light in Arabic.
(Chapter 93)

Below the text of the chapter of the Glorious Morning Light translated to English [9]:

In the Name of Allah, Most Gracious, Most Merciful. By the Glorious Morning Light, And by the Night when it is still, Thy Guardian-Lord hath not forsaken thee, nor is He displeased. And verily the Hereafter will be better for thee than the present. And soon will thy Guardian-Lord give thee (that wherewith) thou shalt be well-pleased. Did He not find thee an orphan and give thee shelter (and care)? And He found thee wandering, and He gave thee guidance. And He found thee in need, and made thee independent. Therefore, treat not the orphan with harshness, Nor repulse the petitioner (Nor repulse him who asks); But the bounty of the Lord - rehearse and proclaim!

Text 8: Chapter of the Glorious Morning Light in English.
(Chapter 93)

In order to facilitate recitation of the chapter of the Glorious Morning Light, I added the below text presenting Arabic pronunciation of this chapter:

Wad-Dhuha. Wal-layli idha saja. Ma wadda'aka rabbuka wa ma qala. Wa la lakhiratu khayrun laka mina l'oula. Wala sawfa yu'ateeka rabbuka fa tardha. Alm yajidka yatiman fa awa. Wa wajadaka dhallan f hada. Wa wajadaka a'ilan fa aghna. Fa amma lyatima fala taq'har. Wa amma assa'ila fala tanhar. Wa amma bi ni'amati rabbika fa haddith.

Text 9: Arabic pronunciation of the chapter of the Glorious Morning Light.
(Chapter 93)

Real stories on the prophet viewing

The real and true stories that I have seen during my dreams explain the prophet Muhammad $_{PBUH}$ viewing for three times in the same year 2013, from March to September.

These three real dreams about the prophet Muhammad $_{PBUH}$ were as follows:

- The first viewing, where I have seen the prophet as a grace or light rain between two so big mountains, was as a preparation for the second and the third viewings;
- The second viewing was about the prophet Muhammad $_{PBUH}$ as a beloved person at a standing position, and with two other persons;
- The third viewing was about the prophet Muhammad $_{PBUH}$ as a beloved person at a sitting position.

Note that these three true dreams were also confirmed during another dream when I was talking about the prophet Muhammad $_{PBUH}$ with my friend "Nureddine". And I told him that I have seen the prophet Muhammad $_{PBUH}$ for three times.

First viewing

One day, I was pronouncing the name of Allah, and the name of his prophet Muhammad $_{PBUH}$, as follows:

- My love is Allah Most High;
- My love Muhammad is the messenger of Allah $_{PBUH}$;
- O God, Allah Most High, I want to see your beloved face;
- ...

After repeating these invocations for many days, and many times. I felt that I pronounce the name of Allah Most High, and that of the prophet Muhammad $_{PBUH}$ respectively, which make confusion in pronouncing.

Following to this issue, I was thinking if it is possible to pronounce only the name of Allah Most High just to avoid confusion of the beloved names of Allah Most High, and his prophet Muhammad $_{PBUH}$ during invocations.

I was thinking for many times in this issue, it was a big problem in my mind. In addition, I was checking at any time this idea by saying, if I do not pronounce the name of the prophet Muhammad $_{PBUH}$, what will I say to Allah Most High, on the Day of Judgment? I have thought only two days in this idea.

On the third day, Allah blessed me by seeing the prophet Muhammad $_{PBUH}$ in dreams as a solution for my issue.

On the fourth day, after the prophet Muhammad $_{PBUH}$ viewing, I decided definitely to pronounce both names of Allah Most High, and his prophet Muhammad $_{PBUH}$ forever.

Here are what I saw in my first true dream:

I saw myself between two big mountains, where I was crying. My body height was almost the same as that of each mountain. It was a wonderful event in my life.

The two mountains were as follows: one behind me, and the other was in front of me.

The weather was cloudy and rainy. I was all time invocating Allah Most High and my tears were getting down. My hands were raised to the sky at the level of my chest. My eyes were directed to the earth at the same level of my hands. I was kneeling down during invocation and all the time of the dream.

While I was crying, I felt and responded myself that the prophet was that event (grace or light rain that was falling on me). During this viewing I was not able to see exactly the beloved body of the prophet Muhammad $_{PBUH}$, but I was sure in my dream by a true feeling that who I saw was the prophet Muhammad $_{PBUH}$ but He $_{PBUH}$ was not clear to me, or we were separated by a barrier which was presented by the raindrops, cloud, and sky.

This dream was only like a preparation of the prophet Muhammad $_{PBUH}$ viewing. When I got-up I was the happiest man in the world. Anything starts to appear very easy to me. I knew that seeing the prophet is a very important dream which can never be from devil according to what the prophet Muhammad $_{PBUH}$ has said in the Hadith.

Being blessed by the grace of Allah Most High and seeing the prophet Muhammad $_{PBUH}$ in dreams is a great and an enormous event that a person can see in his / her life.

All my praise is to my beloved Allah Most High, for the help, the bounty, and the blessings that gave me for the prophet Muhammad $_{PBUH}$ viewing. Moreover, I hope that all people can see the beloved prophet Muhammad $_{PBUH}$.

My first view was only the beginning. Let us see what I viewed in my second and third dreams.

Second viewing

As I had decided to love only my God Allah Most High, and his prophet Muhammad $_{PBUH}$, I changed all the photos of my electronic accounts by one photo that says "I love Allah". This love was coming from my heart.

Seeing the prophet does not mean that the person has never done any sins. However, the smaller the sins are, more the person will be blessed by seeing the prophet Muhammad $_{PBUH}$ in dream if he or she wants.

The prophet Muhammad $_{PBUH}$ viewing is mainly expressed by the love degree, in the person's heart, reserved for Allah Most High and to his prophet Muhammad $_{PBUH}$.

People having already done big sins like illegal sexual relations, drink alcohol, …, should ask forgiveness from Allah before thinking in the prophet Muhammad $_{PBUH}$ viewing.

Once the person is pardoned from Allah, and if he or she does such rituals described above, there will be a big chance to be blessed by the viewing of the prophet Muhammad $_{PBUH}$.

Here are what I saw in my second true dream:

In my second view, I saw the prophet without any barriers but his beloved face was not so clear to me. Logically, if I clearly saw his beloved face, I will draw him in my mind, and this must not be done by respect to the great efforts of the prophet Muhammad $_{PBUH}$ in guiding mankind to the right and the correct way.

My second view was completely different from the first one. I saw the back of the prophet Muhammad $_{PBUH}$; I saw the color of his clothes. There were the prophet Muhammad $_{PBUH}$, two other people who I cannot remember and distinguish, and me.

It was an awesome moment in my life, when I saw the color and the type of clothes, and the height of the prophet Muhammad $_{PBUH}$. His clothes were with a brown color (tanned and darker at 50%).

I hope and I ask Allah that all people will be able to see the prophet Muhammad $_{PBUH}$ and his beloved clothes many times in dreams, and be with Him $_{PBUH}$ in Paradise.

Third viewing

My third view of the prophet Muhammad *PBUH* was more different than the two previous ones.

On 3rd September, 2013, I read the verse of the Throne, the chapter of the Purity of Faith, and some verses of the chapter of the Glorious Morning Light, in Arabic. At Eleven o'clock (p.m.) I called a friend to ask her about the dream that she saw about the prophet Muhammad *PBUH*, but unfortunately her cell was out of service.

After that, I remembered the prophet Muhammad *PBUH* while I was doing some works on my personal computer.

When I went to bed, I remembered the prophet *PBUH*. While I was in a deep sleep, I saw different dreams. The last one was about the prophet Muhammad *PBUH*.

This third view has changed my life to another direction by trying to do the fewest sins in my life, and praying to get the grace from the greatest name of Allah.

Here are what I saw in my third true dream:

The special thing in this dream was the position and the place of the prophet during my dream. He *PBUH* was wearing clothes with the same color that I saw in my second dream. He *PBUH* was sitting on my bed in front of me. I could see his face, but not so clear to avoid drawing Him *PBUH*, and saying that He *PBUH* is like this or that person.

As you may note, the order of my third dream, coincides with the year of my studies at the university (third), and the day of viewing (3rd September). This dream was not come true by chance. It's Allah Most High who creates events. O my God all my praise and thanks to you.

During this dream, the color of the clothes of the prophet Muhammad $_{PBUH}$ was very clear and similar to that I saw during my second viewing. I said during this dream: "By Allah that is the clothes color of the prophet Muhammad $_{PBUH}$". The color was brown (tanned and darker at 50%), similar to that I saw in the second dream. Note that the Satan cannot take image of anything belonging to the prophet Muhammad $_{PBUH}$.

I was very happy when I was seeing Him $_{PBUH}$ in my dream.

Below what I did before going to bed:
- I recited the verse of the Throne in Arabic;
- I recited the chapter of the Purity of Faith in Arabic;
- I recited some verses of the chapter of the Glorious Morning Light in Arabic;
- I remembered Allah Most High, and his prophet Muhammad $_{PBUH}$;
- I did my invocations;
- …

Therefore, anyone who hopes to see the prophet Muhammad in his or her dream should always remember the prophet Muhammad $_{PBUH}$.

Remark: *The viewing of the prophet $_{PBUH}$ is real and true if you feel during the moment of the dream, that who you are seeing is the prophet Muhammad $_{PBUH}$. Because no devil or Satan can create realities about Muhammad $_{PBUH}$ in dreams.*

Benefits of the prophet viewing

Most of the people hope to see the prophet Muhammad $_{PBUH}$ in dreams, because this viewing has many benefits for the soul and the moral state.

The most important thing at the prophet $_{PBUH}$ viewing is the blessing. However, people who are blessed from Allah Most High, by viewing his prophet Muhammad $_{PBUH}$ in dream can reach easily the lowest score of errors a day, and after that get the grace from the greatest name of Allah.

Moreover, people with the Greatest Name of Allah can use the obtained grace to cure people from health problems with no medicines but by reciting the verse which contains the Greatest Name. This is only one part of the grace.

The prophet Muhammad $_{PBUH}$ was a mercy and a grace from Allah Most High, especially to the mankind. He $_{PBUH}$ told people to believe in Allah Most High, and to follow the correct way, so as to enter paradise after death.

Note that all the prophets were chosen by Allah to guide mankind to the divine path. They faced many difficulties and suffered severe hardships in their efforts to call their erring people to obey and worship the One God, Allah Most High [11].

So, let us hope all to be blessed from Allah Most High, and see the prophet Muhammad $_{PBUH}$ in real dreams. There is nothing more beneficial than the blessing of Allah and the view of the prophet Muhammad $_{PBUH}$.

Conclusion

The viewing of the prophet $_{PBUH}$ is real and true if you feel during the moments of the dream, that who you are seeing is the prophet Muhammad $_{PBUH}$, you are really seeing him, because no devil can create realities about Muhammad $_{PBUH}$ in dreams.

In addition, the viewing of the prophet Muhammad $_{PBUH}$ must be confirmed in an another dream, so as to be sure that there is no doubt that who you saw is the prophet Muhammad $_{PBUH}$, as a blessing from Allah Most High.

My viewing was real and I hope that you will be able to see the prophet Muhammad $_{PBUH}$ several times during your life, and to be with Him $_{PBUH}$ after death.

Note that the less sins people do, the more they will be blessed, the more likely they will see the prophet Muhammad $_{PBUH}$ in their lives. In other words, people should be moralized by the greatest names of Allah as adjectives.

References

[1] Muhammad Ahmed Qadri. Blessings on the Prophet Muhammad PBUH. An important work on the meaning, relevance and importance of sending blessings and greetings on the best of creation. Edition of 2004, Islamic Educational & Cultural Research Center, USA; 2004.

[2] Hasan Qaribullah. The millennium biography of Muhammad. The prophet of Allah. Umm Durman Islamic University and Sammania Grand Shaykh. December 10th, 2013 (http://www.mclean.faithweb.com/Islam.html).

[3] Al-Imam Ibn Kathir. Stories of the Prophets. Translated by Muhammad Mustapha Geme'ah, Al-Azhar. Ad-Damishqi 700-774 H. Published by DARUSSALAM Riyadh, Saudi Arabia.

[4] Ahmad Muhammad El Howfy. Studies in Islam series. Why the prophet Muhammad married more than one. The supreme council for Islamic affairs, Cairo, Arab Republic of Egypt, 1414-1993. (Translated by Ahmad Ibrahim El Orfaly)

[5] The wives of the Messenger of Allah PBUH. Translated by Ali Carrerage. Published by Dar Al-Ghadd Al-Gadeed, Translation & Publishing house. Egypt, Al-Mansoura, 2001.

[6] English dictionary. Dicos Encarta, 2009.

[7] Imran N. Hosein. Ansari Memorial Series. Dreams in Islam. A window to truth and to the heart. Published by Masjid Darul Qur'an long island, New York, USA, 2001.

[8] Islam Awareness. Verse of the Throne. August 23rd, 2013 (http://www.islamawareness.net/Dua/kursi.html).

[9] The Holy Quran. English Translation of the Meanings by Abdullah Yusuf Ali. Formatting by William B. Brown. From a version revised by the Presidency of Islamic Researches, IFTA, Call and Guidance. Published and Printed by the King Fahd Holy Quran Printing Complex in 1987.

[10] Wahiduddin. Living from the Heart. August 24th, 2013 (http://wahiduddin.net/quran/ikhlas.htm).

[11] Abul Hasan Ali Nadwi. MUHAMMAD The Last Prophet A Model For All Time. Edition 2008, Academy of Islamic Research and Publications, Tagore Merg Nadwatul Ulema, Lucknow, India; 2008.

List of texts

Text 1: Verse of the Throne in Arabic. 21

Text 2: Verse of the Throne in English. 22

Text 3: Arabic pronunciation of Throne verse. 22

Text 4: Chapter of the Purity of Faith in Arabic. 25

Text 5: Chapter of the Purity of Faith in English. 26

Text 6: Arabic pronunciation of the chapter of the Purity of Faith. 26

Text 7: Chapter of the Glorious Morning Light in Arabic. 27

Text 8: Chapter of the Glorious Morning Light in English. 28

Text 9: Arabic pronunciation of the chapter of the Glorious Morning Light. 28

www.ingramcontent.com/pod-product-compliance
Lightning Source LLC
Chambersburg PA
CBHW030306030426
42337CB00012B/613